How to
Handle With Care

How to Handle With Care

Working Suggestions from
Across the United States

Wendy L. Samford, Ph.D.

To order additional copies of this book, contact:
Xlibris
844-714-8691
www.Xlibris.com
Orders@Xlibris.com
830319

CONTENTS

Preface

I first came across the Handle With Care (HWC) program while in a training Webex for the Guardian ad Litem[1] program. When I heard the presentation, I started to cry; it literally struck my heart and I knew right then that I had to do everything in my power to bring HWC to my county, my state, my country. That is how forceful hearing about this program hit me, and I am not alone.

Handle with Care is simple—if the police are called to a home where there are children present, they send a notice to the school that says "Handle with Care." That message is distributed to school personnel that encounter that child before the bell rings the very next day. They know something traumatic happened to that child the night prior and to handle that child with extra care. It's that simple. A deeper dive into the program is presented in the first chapter, but that is the premise of the program: communication and kindness to keep kids succeeding in school.

I am writing this little book for two reasons:

1. I received my Ph.D. in Curriculum and Instruction[2] in 2013 and never had one class on trauma sensitive education. Not in

---

[1] CASA/GAL, Court Appointed Special Advocates, Guardians ad Litem for Children, Retrieved 12-7-22, https://nationalcasagal.org/our-work/the-casa-gal-model/.

[2] Samford, W. (2013). Exploring sustained change in teachers' beliefs after professional development. (Doctoral Dissertation, Kent State University).

undergraduate, graduate, or doctoral coursework were there any classes on childhood trauma or what to do about it. That is wrong. Educators need to be informed and armed to handle this very real epidemic and this program provides the professional development that is critical in meeting that need.

2. Since becoming interested in implementing this program, I have spent a great deal of time in conferences, Zoom calls, meetings, and chats with people from all over the United States asking the same question about Handle With Care; "How do I get started?" With the assistance of others who have gone before me, I want to help people answer that question.

Unfortunately, there is no step-by-step diagram, no "one size fits all" answer to that question. The program is designed to fit the needs of individual communities. As you will come to find out in the first chapter, this grass-roots effort has very straight-forward protocol in place to support the fidelity of the program, but how you go about achieving that goal is very individualized. So how can you possibly write a How-To manual without a road map? A bit like driving without a GPS!

I believe the answer to that question is to present how people in other states, counties, schools, and precincts have gone about implementing their programs. This little book presents many ways to implement HWC so that you can borrow bits and pieces that work, or avoid those that do not, in order to set up your own program that best suits your individual needs. "How to Handle With Care" takes a code of fidelity for HWC implementation, and presents diverse ways that others in the United States have made it their own. It is literally a collage of ingenuity that hopefully will spark ideas for implementation in your own community.

This book is small purposefully so that you can read it quickly, and move forward. It gives contact information so that you know you have the support of others who have gone where you are now. You are not alone. As with the start-up of any program, it is a difficult, often uphill battle to get the pieces and players in place to begin the program. Fear of legal ramifications, bureaucratic roadblocks that hinder forward movement, technical barriers, professional development intricacies, and questions about privacy are only a few roadblocks that seem to delay the journey. This book can answer many of those questions so you can see what others all over the United States have done to drive through barriers and arrive at the destination: a successful program supporting the mental health of our kids.

The people who volunteered to share their stories of implementation of this program maneuvered through the storm facing all these fears as they lead implementation of HWC. Even in blizzard like conditions when visibility seemed to be at zero, these people plowed ahead to make a path for others. Why? Because HWC is worth the effort.

"And let us not be weary in well doing, for in due season we shall reap, if we faint not."[3]

---

[3]   New Testament (The). (1989). King James Version Holman Bible Publishers, Galatians 6:9.

Introduction

From 1995 to 1997, the Adverse Childhood Experiences (ACE) study was conducted by Kaiser Permanente[4] on over 17,000 adults in California. Kaiser was looking at a possible correlation between childhood trauma and health deficiencies in adulthood, but an unexpected finding of the study was an extraordinarily high number of people who had been exposed to a traumatic experience as a child. If you are not familiar with the ACE's study, the questions are simple, such as; "Did a household member go to prison?" and "Were your parents ever separated or divorced?" You might want to take a minute to take the test yourself, the results may surprise you.

The sad truth is almost two-thirds of people who participated in the study reported one ACE and one in five replied to the survey that they had experienced three or more ACE's.[5] This high rate of results on the ACE's test begs the question, since research shows that there is a direct correlation between childhood trauma and health (mental and physical) as an adult,[6] if our country elected to place a heavy focus on abuse prevention, how would that affect every citizen in a positive direction?

[4]   U.S. Department of Health and Human Services, The Original ACE Study, Retrieved 12-13-22, https://nhttac.acf.hhs.gov/soar/eguide/stop/adverse_childhood_experiences

[5]   Center for Disease Control and Prevention, About the CDC-Kaiser ACE Study, Retrieved 12-13-22,
https://www.cdc.gov/violenceprevention/aces/about.html

[6]   Van Der Kolk, Bessel. (2014). *The body keeps the score.* Penguin Group.

Common sense would support redirecting our attention in the United States toward preventing child abuse, while simultaneously taking a trauma informed approach immediately after, should childhood trauma occur. Implementing the Handle With Care (HWC) program in our country is a very big step in the right direction.

Chapter 1—The Background of Handle With Care

The Handle With Care program began in 2013 in a small school in West Virginia that was plagued by drugs and violent crime to the extent that the U.S. Attorney's Office created an intervention program in the area to specifically address these two factors. Many years later, this national program not only promotes school and community partnerships, but helps students succeed in school. There are multiple other positive outliers in this program, but ultimately HWC intends to support kids in the school setting who have been traumatized. Andrea Darr is the Co-Founder of Handle With Care and is interviewed in this chapter. She started the HWC program in collaboration with the United States Attorney's Office for the Southern District of West Virginia and key stakeholders in the state of West Virginia, and it has grown into a national program. Andrea shares the origin of the program and lessons learned over years of assisting people nationwide to implement HWC.

Chapter 2—How to Implement Handle With Care
            in Your State

Everyone who has tried to implement HWC in a community can respect the unbelievably hard undertaking it would require to take this program statewide. Through trial and error, Adrienne Elder of Oklahoma shares a fascinating example of doing just that. Through a mindset of reaching into pre-existing programs and filling a need in an organization, the HWC program in this state is spreading from a top-down and bottom-up fashion. Meeting local and state agencies in the middle, the Handle With Care Oklahoma Advisory Committee has left no stone unturned when seeking support, providing support, and/or needing support for this program. Recently, legislation is in place to use HWC as the program to use in various state agencies. With the passage of this House Bill, it will change the face of trauma informed care in this state.

Chapter 3—How to Implement Handle With Care
        in Your County

Implementing statewide, one county at a time describes the state of Ohio's model for HWC. Robyn Venoy is Ohio's HWC Lead and she oversees the counties as they discover and eventually bring the program to fruition in their community. Robyn shares key ingredients that she believes makes their counties' individual implementation run as smoothly as possible. A Training of Trainers model is utilized to build teams of inter-agency volunteers who provide training on the HWC model and support County Coordinators—as it is said, teamwork makes the dream work! The goal in Ohio is: statewide implementation working with each county on their fidelity and timeline, adjusting implementation to fit individual community needs, thus promoting fidelity *and* flexibility!

Chapter 4—How to Implement Handle With Care
        in Your School

HWC meets the kids where they spend most of their day: in school. We know that trauma has a short-term and lasting effect on a child's ability to stay focused, behave in an appropriate manner, and ultimately learn and "often leads to school failure, truancy, suspension, or expulsion, dropping out, or involvement in the juvenile justice system."[7] HWC uses everything we currently know about the effects of trauma and implements trauma informed professional development to all school personnel so that all educators and staff are better informed, thereby equipped to support these children. They may not have to take a test,

---

[7]   West Virginia Center for Children's Justice, Handle With Care. Retrieved 12-13-22, http://www.handlewithcarewv.org/handle-with-care.php

or can be permitted to go to the nurse's office and lay down, or maybe an altercation avoided simply because the teacher is aware there is a problem. Sara Kettwig works through the SD School Safety Center to support communities in South Dakota to successfully implement the HWC program. The creative support for a focus on completely local implementation in schools is unique to their state and this chapter provides an honest look into their initiative.

Chapter 5—How to Implement Handle With Care
              in Your Law Enforcement Agency

This program does not work without the buy-in and support of our first responders, the police officers, and/or sheriffs' deputies in your community. They are the first on the scene and are instrumental in discovering if children are in the home, gathering information on the child's name and age and school, and then sending that information to designated contacts with the school. Without the backing of local law enforcement, the program will not work or, at the very least, will work inconsistently throughout the various communities. In return for complete participation by law enforcement, officers can be assured that when they leave the scene, the children are not being left behind, and someone at school is looking out for that child. Lieutenant Veto Mentzell of Maryland shares how his state implements the HWC program. He talks about changes to the program over his 5-year tenure working with officers to ensure the fidelity of HWC while sharing training tips.

Lessons Learned

What I have learned after conducting all the interviews and writing this book, the HWC program has quickly become a grassroots effort and it is spreading like wildfire. What does it take to start this program in your community? First, form a stakeholder's group and sign a Memorandum of Understanding so you can begin to brainstorm implementation ideas (Who, What, When, Where, Why, and How), and experimenting with various ideas in a program plan is the way to get started in the right direction. Using various tools and data and putting your hypothesis into action, you must be ever mindful to revisit the plan and adjust as needed.

One step in the planning phase that cannot be skipped is to identify the problem and pull together people who are passionate about addressing that problem. Unfortunately, pinpointing the exact problem is sometimes the problem![8] I think we can all agree that the high level of childhood trauma is a national issue, but the identified problem is for the individual community to dig up.

Once you have identified the problem in your community, a change in mindset[9] needs to be addressed. Training and professional development is key in supporting this change. That old saying knowledge is power is true and once your eyes are opened to the problem, you cannot unsee what you saw. Over time, people profess a vested interest in seeing the success of the program. One thing I have seen, if you put the right people in the right places, very little supervision is needed.[10] Passionate people in leadership positions create momentum that cannot be duplicated!

The guarantee for implementing this program is there will be setbacks. As with any program that is grassroots, trial and error is part of the set up so the key is taking the time to create a culture of trust.

> Time to develop trust elicits empathy for each other;
> it opens our minds and our hearts to the possibility of
> new beginnings. With trust, we also open ourselves to
> the possibility of constructive criticism; empathy invites
> differing opinions with the trust that the critique is not
> for harm but for the betterment of all.[11]

---

[8] Gornik, R., & Samford, W. L. (2018) *Creating a culture of support for teacher leaders: A vision for change and hope* (p. 32). Rowman and Littlefield.

[9] Dweck, C. S. (2008). *Mindset: The new psychology of success.* Ballantine Books.

[10] Buckingham, M., & Coffman, C. (1999). *First, break all the rules.* Simon & Schuster.

[11] Samford, W. L. (2016). *Out of the dark: A direction for change in education* (p. 81). Wipf and Stock.

Of course, there must be a strong, strategic game plan for implementation, but as everyone knows who works with children, expect the unexpected. Just remember when you must go back to the drawing board to face whatever adjustments you must make, "There's a crack in everything, that's how the light gets in."[12] Any time you are trying to implement a program that causes change addressing a particular problem, expect the unexpected and create a culture that welcomes ideas for improvement and supports adjustments. From what I have seen, the people who created a sustained change in their state, county, school, and precinct, did just that.

Here are their stories.

---

[12]   Brown, B. (2012) *Daring greatly: How the courage to be vulnerable transforms the way we live, love, parent, and lead* (p. 137). Penguin Random House.

Chapter 1

The Background of Handle With Care

Andrea Darr, Co-Founder Handle With Care
adarr@jbsinternational.com

Until a few years ago, there was no funding stream for Handle With Care (HWC); we just simply wrote it into our job description. That is amazing, but that is how this program runs. It's not the money that makes this program run—it's the people, and it started out as just an idea.

The Idea

The whole program started as a partnership between the WV Children's Justice Task Force and the U.S. Attorney's Office. In early 2011, my friend called me to see if we could work together to address children's exposure to crime, violence, and abuse. At the time, the Defending Childhood Initiative[13] was launched throughout the country and I, as the coordinator for the WV Children's Justice Task Force, was interested in being a part of that initiative. As a child victim advocate working for the state of West Virginia, I immediately said "Yes" to her

---

[13] U.S. Department of Justice Archives, Defending Childhood. Retrieved 1-25-2023, from https://www.justice.gov/archives/defendingchildhood

request and we started planning. A subcommittee was formed and we began monthly meetings focusing on a national survey[14] that stated more than 60% of all children had been exposed to violence in the past year. Childhood exposure to violence was the topic we explored, and we knew we needed to learn more.

In the summer of 2011, we heard about a program called the Red Envelope Project, spearheaded by Ed Jacoubs from Plymouth County, Massachusetts, and we invited him to speak at our fall multi-disciplinary conference on child maltreatment. The Red Envelope Project included a notification from law enforcement to the school anytime children were present on a domestic call. Our committee knew that their idea was good, but we also knew our main problems in WV were with drugs and poverty, therefore our program would have to address all possible forms of trauma in children. We started working with the Trauma and Learning Policy Initiative[15] and so began a deep dive into learning about childhood trauma. The books, "Helping Traumatized Children Learn" Parts I and II,[16] quickly became a necessary read for all of our committee members.

In the beginning, the program ideas looked very different than the culminating result. At first, it was much broader in scope. But because there were so many different disciplines at the table with so many different policies and procedures, we had to keep cutting parts of the program. For instance, "We can't do this because it violates confidentiality." "We can't do this because it might jeopardize victim safety." "We can't do this because it violates my policy, might not violate yours, but it violates mine."

---

[14]   U.S. Department of Justice, *OJJDP National Survey of Children's Exposure to Violence.* Retrieved 1-6-23, from https://www.ojp.gov/pdffiles1/ojjdp/227744.pdf

[15]   Trauma and Learning Policy Initiatives. *Helping traumatized children learn.* Retrieved 1-25-2023, from https://traumasensitiveschools.org/about-tlpi/

[16]   Cole, S., Gregory, M., Greenwald-O'Brien, J., Gadd, G., Ristuccia, J., & Wallace, L. (2005), Helping traumatized children learn (Volume I). Massachusetts Advocates for Children, MA. Retrieved 1-25-2023, from https://traumasensitiveschools.org/tlpi-publications/

All of the exhaustive research, intense meetings, and hard work paid off because by 2012, we had whittled the program down to three little words, Handle With Care (HWC).[17] All of the discussion caused us to stick to our program simplicity divulging no information, no details; just three words. You don't need to know the details; you just have to understand trauma. We started big and ended small and concise. We shaved the rough edges, refining the main mission and in the end, HWC became more than an idea. At this point we agreed, if HWC worked in our heads, it was time to see if it worked in the field.

The Pilot

One thing was clear, we all knew that we had to get all school staff involved for this program to work. HWC is a whole school approach, and schools are the perfect point of intervention because kids are mandated to go to school and have transportation to get there. Kids spend the majority of their day at school and school staff usually know a great deal about their kids. For some children, school is the only place where they feel safe, have their basic needs meet, and have access to connections with caring adults. School is also the best place to receive mental health services for children who need the services and for those whose caregivers give their permission for the services.

In January 2013, Mary C. Snow Elementary School in Charleston, WV, was chosen to be the pilot for HWC. The school is in an urban area and had the highest reports of violent crime and, at the time, served approximately 500 students. The school performance ranking was 398 out of 404 elementary schools in the state. It seemed to be perfect for what we were seeking, a school where HWC could possibly make a difference.

---

[17]   West Virginia Center for Children's Justice, Handle With Care. Retrieved 1-7-23, from http://www.handlewithcarewv.org/

As fate would have it, the program landed in the lap of Lieutenant Chad Napier.[18] Lieutenant Napier had extensive experience with the Metro Drug Unit conducting and/or supervising drug investigations. He took on the pilot program. Unfortunately, as new programs seem to web and flow, three months into the program, he got a call from the school nurse stating that not one HWC notice had come in since January. This officer simply said, "This is not going to fail on my watch" and promptly started checking every police report to see if a child was present, and if so, was the notice sent. When the officers realized that HWC was a priority in the department and that their reports were being checked, the notices began flowing. Maybe the first thing on the officers' minds were safety and doing the job that they knew. Maybe when the officers saw that the program was important to leadership, they began to see its merit. Maybe they just didn't understand, early in the program, the effects of trauma on children. Whatever the reason, once they got it, they got it, and it became part of their routine.

Program Expansion

In 2014, we decided to expand the program and worked tirelessly expanding one county at a time. There were starts and stalls too many to count, but Lieutenant Napier, the United States Attorney, myself, and our team forged ahead. There are 55 counties in WV and over the next two years, together we went to every county. Some figured it out quickly and others started the program before we even got there. Still, others we had to visit multiple times before the program caught on. We never went anywhere that did not ask for the program, but once people heard about HWC, they wanted to bring it to their county.

In the beginning we made mistakes, but we always learned from them. For instance, at first, we told the officers if they thought the kids were traumatized send a notice. We realized that police officers are used to trauma and their gauge for judging what that means is very

---

[18]   YouTube, Handle With Care, Chad Napier. Retrieved 1-2-23, from https://www.youtube.com/watch?v=-P_qnbVkR8c

individualized. We quickly changed the directive to if any children are present, send the notice. We learned from experience as we grew, acknowledging the good, the bad, and the ugly, and making changes as needed.

At the time we were starting our program, people from other states were hearing about our initiative and began to be curious. The United Hospital Fund in NYC reached out to include HWC in a discussion they were planning around children in the opioid crisis.[19] The next thing I knew, I was in New York City to be a part of a larger discussion and was given a 7 minute platform to explain HWC. Little did I know that because of a delayed plane, one of the speakers on day one was unable to make their time slot and I was asked to improvise in their place. Was I nervous? You bet, but this change of fate afforded our little program the opportunity to shine. Running out of time near the end of the presentation, I just blurted out: "The last thing you want to do is jump ugly on a kid who has been traumatized." The commissioner came up to me at the end of the day and thanked me for bringing that catch phrase to NYC.

Soon after that presentation, HWC just took off. We were trying to get the program up and running in our own counties while receiving calls from all over the U.S. asking how to get their programs started. I have to say it was like building the plane while we were flying it.

HWC Takes Flight

My job, as program manager of the WV Center for Children's Justice, is to provide the technical support for HWC, conduct quarterly meetings, sponsor the yearly, multi-disciplinary conference, and really everything else that needs addressed to support the state and nationwide

---

[19] The Ripple Effect (*The Ripple Effect: The Impact of the Opioid Epidemic on Children and Families, United Hospital Fund*. Retrieved 1-25-2023, from https://uhfnyc.org/media/filer_public/59/b2/59b20ad0-6acf-4980-ba9a-07ad5f565386/uhf-opioids-20190307.pdf

spread of this program. It is so important that the fidelity of the program is kept.[20]

One very important component of implementation is common understanding of the problem. I discovered early on that everyone has their own perspective about the drug crisis. If you talk to police about drugs, they think about arrests and overcrowding in the jails. If you talk to an emergency first responder about drugs, they will think about the high rate of overdoses and the administration of NARCAN.[21] Ask a public health provider and they think about the spread of Hepatitis and increase in HIV cases and ask anyone in child welfare, and they think about removal of children and not enough beds. Depending on the field, everyone comes at the same topic from a different angle. This is not bad, just different, but we must be willing to discuss these differences with a common language to finally get to what is best for kids.

Children need safety, support, and access to caring adults if they are going to be successful in school and in life. The bottom line is, we must all come to a consensus on how trauma affects a child's ability to focus, to behave appropriately, and to learn. Many kids live in neglectful and abusive situations and having a trauma informed school is the key to reaching those children. After all, behavior is communication and although we might see "bad" behavior in children, sometimes it's the only way they know to communicate. Kids who need the most love often ask for that attention in the most unloving ways.

Everything I do is about the investigation, prosecution, and resolution of child maltreatment cases. We want to respond better and faster, have better outcomes for kids, and do it in a way that does not cause further harm. We must all work together in the best interest of the children and HWC helps this process all fall into place. We have

---

[20]   West Virginia Center for Children's Justice. *How to Get HWC Started in my County*. Retrieved 2-10-23, from http://www.handlewithcarewv.org/get-hwc-started.php

[21]   National Institute on Drug Abuse. *Naloxone Drug Facts*. Retrieved 2-10-23, from https://nida.nih.gov/publications/drugfacts/naloxone

recently created a Handle With Care Mandated Reporter Course[22] and already 4,700 people have participated in the training. Interestingly, so many professions are mandatory reporters, but so many people don't really know how to recognize child abuse and neglect and how to report. This and other training videos are available for anyone at any time.

Today

Today our focus is not only statewide but nationally, implementing a trauma informed response to child maltreatment and children's exposure to violence. I am involved in multiple organizations and initiatives all across the United States and my goal is spreading the HWC program to as many communities, counties, and states as possible. In order to achieve this goal, I have to be well informed and up-to-speed on what is taking place in the field. This is imperative if you want to come up with current interventions for the kids.

Our monthly meetings (currently the third Thursday of every month) attract people from all over the country. Some attendees are just interested in hearing more about HWC, some people have questions about starting up a program in their community, and still others have already implemented and are successfully running the program in their schools, precincts, counties, and states. Routinely, this meeting is attended by 50–100 people and I try to make them informative, yet with enough wiggle room for people to learn from each other.

I must say, implementation in our state may have been easier than in many others. Each of our counties only has one school district. Therefore, providing we have a point of contact in each county that can receive and send the notice to the proper school, our communication link is simple. And if it is simple, it is more likely to happen. We have a volunteer coordinator in every county, usually in the school, to collect and forward the notice and to report the number of notifications each month by county.

---

[22]   West Virginia Center for Children's Justice. Mandated Reporter Course. Retrieved 1-25-2023, from http://www.handlewithcarewv.org/

We have found that the officers on the front line have to be on board for this program to work and leadership within the agency has to make it a priority. We try to always reinforce that notices are sent all year round. The schools need to know if some kids had problems over the summer and it keeps the officers in the habit of reporting. There is, however, flexibility on how the notice is sent. Some first responder agencies have someone to check the reports and send out the notice. In small counties, everyone knows everyone and has their cell number, so they just give them a call or text at the school. Some counties use dispatch to send the notices. However, after the notice is sent, the schools are the main support for the fidelity of the HWC. The training, and more importantly, the comprehension of the effects of trauma on children is imperative to the quality of the program that you have in your community.

Lastly, having access to mental health services for children who need these services is essential. Many times, parents cannot get their kids to appointments for a number of reasons. Maybe they are working 2 or 3 jobs to pay the bills and can't take time off, maybe transportation is an issue, and maybe there are other children in the home that make leaving impossible. Whatever the reason, that is why we want services available on site with care giver permission. We recommend Trauma Focused Cognitive Behavioral Therapy (TF-CBT) as the modality for intervention and each school should know what services are available in their community and be able to have access to that information. Point being, once you identify specific needs of children and families, it is so very important to be able to direct them to the resources available for assistance in each community. The bottom line is these resources are offered for all families and all children.

On a bigger scale, the goal shouldn't be HWC for one child. If you do it right, you help all kids; the ones we know have experienced trauma and the ones suffering in silence. Maybe all of us will become just a little bit kinder and as a result, so will our kids.

On the National Level

As this book goes to print, we are pleased to announce the National Handle with Care Program. I am proud to be named the HWC Subject Matter Expert at JBS International[23] and look forward to seeing how HWC expands with this full-time national support system in place. It is my pleasure to work in this program and support all the many people who seek to see that HWC is implemented nationwide, one small community at a time.

---

[23]   JBS International: A Celerian Group Company. Retrieved 7-6-23, from https://www.jbsinternational.com/

Chapter 2

How to Implement Handle With Care in Your State

Adrienne B. Elder, MPH, Director of Early Intervention,
Public Health Institute of Oklahoma
Adrienne@publichealthok.org

My background is in public health, so when I first heard of Handle With Care (HWC) in West Virginia from reading a PACEs Connection website article, I was immediately drawn to the interagency collaboration to help children/youth after a traumatic event. After twenty years in the field and five years of promoting and implementing HWC, it is rejuvenating to pause and reflect on the progress we have made together in Oklahoma. Once you see this program and you say, "We've got to do this," you can't undo it! It is a lifelong calling for me and at the end of the day, I hope to say that I tried to move things down the road and made a difference with an amazing team of people.

A simple illustration we use to explain our statewide interagency planning and implementation is to picture a long hallway with closed doors along both sides. You are walking down the hallway and you stop and knock on a door. If the door doesn't open, do you stand there and keep knocking? No. There are so many pathways to implement this program, so if one door is locked, we try another. There are always doors opening and closing, so as long as we persist, there is always an opportunity for entering into a new partnership and enhancing the initiative. We recommend doing your best to be inclusive and invite everyone to be a part of the program. When a door opens, quit knocking and wasting time on the locked one. Maybe they just aren't ready to open up yet.

When we started the challenge of statewide planning and implementation, we explored the idea of mandating the program across the state of Oklahoma. The problem with that direction is that the two most overburdened occupations happen to be schools and law enforcement agencies. When we discussed a HWC mandate, people in these occupations were so overwhelmed and perceived the program to be one more directive crammed on their already full plates. When we went to them to say, "Do one more thing," they simply said, "We can't." After some reflection, and a lot of locked doors we adjusted our statewide approach.

Increasing Awareness

After piloting Handle With Care at the local level with Oklahoma City Police Department (OCPD) and Oklahoma City Public Schools (OKCPS), we created a small training team with a law enforcement perspective, a school perspective, and a community perspective. With this unique mix of backgrounds, we made statewide presentations at conferences, community meetings, and the sheriff's academy. As we increased awareness and asked for community feedback, there was a groundswell of support because everyone felt a connection to this effort. Finally, the community coalitions felt like this program could enhance their current efforts and increase collaboration.

The lightbulb moment was when we looked at what already existed and focused on how HWC could enhance partnerships. There is no need to start from scratch. It takes time to build relationships among multiple levels of influence, highlight shared goals, and increase alignment to make all the gears work. This collaborative mindset helped create a roadmap for all communities to increase stability at school, at home, and in the community. Now we know you have to get your community organizations on board, get the word out there, and create a parallel path with pre-existing programs. Having community buy-in creates positive momentum for implementation. This shift in approach has enhanced our existing partnerships and strengthened collaboration in programs across the state.

Now, we are building interagency relationships based on trust that includes a framework for trauma informed communities whereby HWC is one piece of that puzzle. We had to look for the other missing pieces that complement efforts.

What does that look like for individual communities and statewide efforts? It looks like a strength-based approach between all agencies at every level, from state to local and everything in between. The way to look at implementation now is to ask, "What existing programs do you have and how does HWC fit into that program?" With that direction, there is more of a unified team working together to enhance pre-existing programs with support if they need it. Statewide training is available, but not mandatory because individual communities know they are already driving the bus; they might just need to pull over and pick up some additional team members along the way.

The Oklahoma Way—Enhancing Partnerships

HWC begins with a simple notice by law enforcement to the schools, but community partnerships must be in place, so that coordinated services are available for the behavioral health of children and families. We now know in order to create trauma informed communities, that there must be a wrap-around support already in place for HWC to work at its highest level of success. Rather than put the cart before the horse, you have a plan in place that can be immediately implemented if/when a child or their family needs additional help beyond classroom kindness and school resources. With this mindset, schools are aware of the various organizations that are available even before a child needs additional support, and a plan has been established that directs attention when and where it is needed, at school or at home.

Implementation of trauma informed communities statewide works any way that is best for your individual community needs. You might want to start with community strengths, or if you already have a relationship with state agencies, open that door. What we have found is that it works best if we work both directions, local and state working together as a team. If one gets ahead of the other, problems occur. For example; if the school gets ahead of the state, they are on their own with little support. If the state moves too far ahead of the community, the local level resists overreach and mandates. Through trial and error and creating a culture of trust, this program amplifies progress.

Our focus now is to create trauma-informed communities that realize, recognize, and respond to the needs of our communities. We promote interagency hope-centered and trauma-informed trainings (ex., NEAR Science) that focus on what organizations are already doing and incorporate HWC into their training. If a particular agency is focusing on youth trauma, we focus on that topic. If an agency is focused on addiction, we start with addiction. Trainings start simple, but eventually uncover what is lacking and uncover opportunities to further strengthen each community. Universally when the trauma trainings are over, people ask, "Ok now what?" "What can we do to address this problem" and the answer is pretty clear that HWC is one way to address that need. Why? Because implementation is simple. When you take the time to start serious talks together with a common understanding, the foundation of that relationship is built on unity and trust.

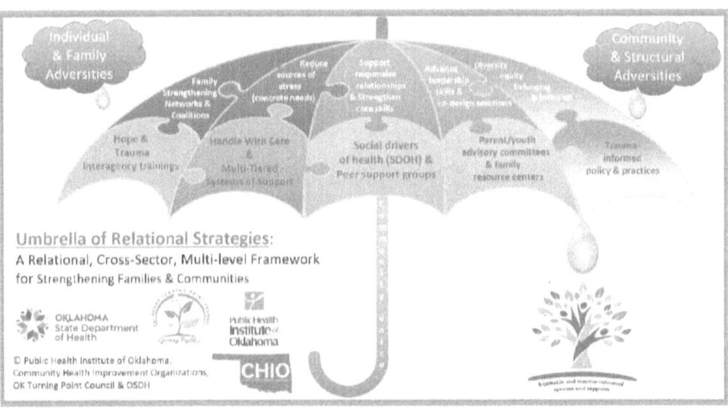

This umbrella visual was co-created with individuals who not only had traumatic experiences, but had buffering supports to heal and recover. They wanted an image that showed how Handle With Care, along with other complementing strategies, is essential to address individual, family, and community adversities. As schools utilize multi-tiered systems of support (MTSS) to meet the needs of their students, including children who have received a Handle With Care notification, we noticed that support groups were often another missing piece. When families need additional care, support groups can create a safe space for a positive social network to develop and grow. These groups can happen at school or community resource centers and they become a springboard to getting families back on track. They are a pathway for healing and recovery. Many times, when people graduate from these groups, they have lived experience in recovery and they can be perfect candidates to help create community solutions. Support group graduates become a pipeline to be on a parent or youth advisory committee to give feedback on barriers that the community needs to prioritize. They then provide possible solutions, along with community leaders, that are relevant to the people who need the support.

With these pieces in place, our system is improving at a faster pace. All involved stakeholders are trying to work together to create trauma informed policies and procedures that allow the caregiver/youth to access supports, as needed.

Getting Started—Building Relationships

Getting started with the new mindset of developing trauma informed communities was not easy. One early snag was getting all the agencies to let go of some control and be honest and open about their limitations. In order to recognize that you need assistance, you must be vulnerable about your needs and be willing to pass authority to another agency. For instance, law enforcement must say, "I can't be the social worker, but I can inform the school that something traumatic happened to this child." Schools need to be able to say, "This child needs more specialized services than we have available, but I can communicate with a local mental health agency." Lastly, behavior health or social services need to know their limitations and have recommendations for other agencies that might be a better fit for the child's individual needs. In order for this direction to work, partnership agreements help memorialize what initially started as trust and communication.

Soon after we adjusted our direction for implementation from mandated to improved communication, we knew we needed a backbone agency to support us. We partnered with the Public Health Institute of Oklahoma[24] (PHIO) because when they were approached with the prospect of the HWC program, they opened the door wide open and simply asked, "What do you need?" We did a presentation at their Oklahoma Turning Point statewide conference and the leaders jumped on board. Later we submitted an interim study to present at the Capitol and organized a team of interagency leaders to attend the national HWC conference together. With this foundation in place, PHIO became the statewide designated lead for HWC. These relationships that were gleaned at the onset of the program development became the backbone that held the body together.

With ongoing guidance from Andrea Darr from West Virginia and the success of her national meetings, we established a statewide advisory team and continue to hold monthly virtual planning meetings. If people were able to attend, they did and if there was a conflict, they sent a representative. Developing these relationships turned out to be invaluable. If something needed clarification or we hit a snag, I could contact the state representative, and the door suddenly opened. The development of those relationships was imperative to moving forward in our state.

At the same time, we were developing honest relationships with communities that already had HWC in place. The monthly meetings are a venue for consistent communication as to what is working and what is not working. The communication we received from law enforcement officials and school personnel was imperative to moving the program

---

[24] Public Health Institute of Oklahoma. Retrieved 2-22-2023, from https://publichealthok.org/

forward in other communities. Trial and error in programming was expected and supported.

I started listing action steps after each meeting, with the idea, who suggested the idea, were there any actions to be taken, in what timeframe, and by whom. Each meeting I listen to community partners and prioritize suggestions. As they are completed, they are crossed off the list so other suggestions can be added and completed. There was no pressure and always room for people to join the conversation because in this format, there are always open action steps. Either I could complete an action step or someone who just joined the meeting for the first time could complete the step in their community. The process was and is innovative and inclusive. Sometimes you can step up, and sometimes you cannot. The point is you are never stuck and everyone is involved.

After the meetings, minutes were sent out with the action steps. This held me accountable and everyone else. Sometimes there was a deadline; sometimes it was just an open "ongoing" timeline. The point is, all ideas were noted, and most were assigned which kept the conversation real and doable. We keep up with this format to this day.

At the beginning, we weren't holding virtual meetings. Oddly, Covid pushed everything into virtual meetings so it forced people to communicate on-line. This afforded me the opportunity to attend multiple state meetings without ever traveling. I made a calendar with the meetings for each organization and made it a point to attend each one. By doing so, I could hear what their priorities were and I could line my request up with their pre-existing programs. The doors began to open in multiple agencies and I gladly walked in each one.

For example, the Certified Community Behavioral Health Clinics[25] (CCBHC) had been working with small cohorts of schools and each year they were expanding with the Oklahoma Department of Mental Health and their Behavioral Support Services Schools (BISS). I started attending their meetings and they started attending ours and we decided

---

[25]   Oklahoma Mental Health and Substance Abuse. Certified Community Behavioral Health Clinics. Retrieved 2-22-2023, from https://oklahoma.gov/odmhsas/treatment/ccbhc.html

to collaborate. They were addressing trauma in the school and so were we. Over time, they incorporated HWC into one of their strategies. It took a few years, but in staying with our approach to integrate this program into existing programs, it just worked. Before we knew it, the Oklahoma Department of Human Services[26] (OKDHS) hired school based social workers which turned out to be just another opportunity to network and support the implementation of HWC in the schools. It is all beginning to fit.

Today—Ongoing Statewide Planning

Today things are going much more smoothly than in the beginning. I worked for a few years just as a volunteer because I knew I wanted to implement this program in my state. Hard work and perseverance pay off. Last year, we wrote and received The Health Disparities Planning Grant[27] through the Oklahoma State Department Of Health (OSDH). Basically, a Covid-19 recovery grant, our justification focused on the great deal of unaddressed trauma because of the pandemic and we needed an increase in interagency efforts to address this problem. We focused on interagency strategies (like the umbrella visual previously mentioned), where HWC is part of the grant, but not the focus. It is more of a "menu of options" when people ask the question, "What can we do about the trauma in our community?"

Over the years, our relationship with the Public Health Institute of Oklahoma and Oklahoma Turning Point has grown. With the support and guidance of Andrea Darr, Co-Founder of Handle With Care West Virginia, PHIO purchased the HWC website template[28] that keeps

---

26 Oklahoma Human Services. Retrieved 2-22-2023, from https://oklahoma.gov/okdhs.html

27 Oklahoma State Department of Health, Covid 19 Disparity Grant. Retrieved 2-22-2023, from https://oklahoma.gov/covid19/resources-recommendations/covid19-disparities-grant.html

28 Handle With Care Oklahoma. Retrieved 2-22-2023, from https://handlewithcareok.org/

with the national fidelity of the program. Other key organizational steps include creating a statewide advisory shared Google drive where everything we do is captured and transparency is expected. This backbone support has been essential to our success and growth.

We continue to rely on our statewide virtual meetings on the first Wednesday of every month. All counties are welcome to attend and encouraged to do so. The first 20–30 minutes we do introductions/questions and we track all of those concerns and celebrate all of the accomplishments. During the second half of the meeting, we bring in speakers to offer resources and support for concerns that were identified at the previous month's meeting. There is a constant flow of give and take that is targeted to exact needs continuously being met. This is helpful especially for communities that are just starting or are in a silo and are not yet heavily supported.

Although we initially started with a plan to mandate HWC, we now spend our time building relationships with agencies and organizations in as many of our 77 counties as we can reach. To date, it has taken us 5 years to work with schools in 35 of our 77 counties. Our goal is to have a statewide process in place when the majority of our counties are in full implementation of the program. We are working toward that goal with open communication, one relationship at a time.

Legislation and Systems Change

In May of 2022, House Bill 4106[29] passed that required all schools to have a partnership agreement with a community mental health center to provide support services. With the passage of this bill, there is a much smoother transition to implementing the HWC program because the schools have the behavioral health supports in place for their students.

After the school shooting in Uvalde, Texas, Oklahoma's Governor signed an executive order (Mission S.O.S.: Secure Oklahoma Schools) on June 22, 2023. This included requiring the Oklahoma School

---

[29] Oklahoma State Legislature, Bill Information for HB 4106. Retrieved 2-22-2023, from http://www.oklegislature.gov/BillInfo.aspx?Bill=hb4106&Session=2200

Security Institute (OSSI) to make available to every public and private primary and secondary school a risk and vulnerability assessment.

Presently, we have been working diligently on legislation that would support the HWC program, address the legality of the program, and create a streamlined training process. Legislation addressing legal issues will alleviate beginning implementation concerns that consistently need attention. With this bill, we will save hours of unnecessary concern on the part of local schools, law enforcement, and behavioral health agencies.

In the spring of 2023, House Bill 2513[30] unanimously passed the House Common Education Committee 11-0, passed the House Floor 94-0, passed the Senate Education Committee 12-0, and passed the Senate Floor 42-0! Unfortunately, the governor declined to sign the bill and it was pocket vetoed. We will try again next year.

This bill will not mandate the implementation of HWC, but instead, support certain state agencies to include this program in their existing training. For example: The Oklahoma School Security Institute (OSSI), which is a division of Oklahoma's Office of Homeland Security, already mandates behavioral threat assessment trainings at all schools. Because OSSI is already contracted to do these assessments, they see HWC as an upstream approach to the continuum of care in their already mandated training. The good news, they will be the lead on training all law enforcement in HWC.

Joining OSSI was a huge win for us and this literally just transpired in February of this year. Five years in the making and then out of the blue, they appeared. Honestly, finding agency support for HWC has been like a treasure hunt where you are always searching and then you uncover a hidden gem. Our determination and perseverance will always be driven by the desire to help children in times of need.

---

[30]   Oklahoma State Legislature, Bill Information for HB 2513. Retrieved 7-5-23, from http://www.oklegislature.gov/BillInfo.aspx?Bill=HB2513&Session=2300

Chapter 3

How to Implement Handle With Care in Your County

Robyn Venoy, LISW, Ohio Handle With Care Lead
Robyn.Venoy@hoepwellhealth.org

You won't hear the same message on how to implement Ohio Handle With Care[31] (OhioHWC) as you would in Texas. That is what is so great about this program; it is different in every state, every county, every community. The fidelity is there, but the process varies across the board.

As a former child therapist, I have worked a great deal in the schools and with teachers, and if truth be told, there were times I just couldn't sleep. I guess I did not realize how bad the world could be to innocent kids. Teachers kept asking the same question, "How do we control what happens outside of the school?" My answer was always the same; while it is true that we cannot change what happens at home, we can control what happens in the school. With that focus, I left my role as a therapist and began providing support and training for school staff as a Trauma Informed Care Consultant. Recognizing that we cannot change what happens at home, the goal of consultation is to shift the culture and

---

[31]   Handle With Care Ohio: Protect, Heal, Thrive. Retrieved 1-11-23, from https://www.handlewithcareoh.org/

structure to better support students and staff through Trauma Informed Care (TIC) at every level within the school system.

One thing I noticed early on when providing training was that trauma can be perceived on a wide spectrum. If we consider poverty a potential trauma, some people feel they have experienced poverty because they never went to Disney on vacation or did not have brand-name clothes. Yet, another person's poverty may have been that they grew up without enough food or heat because of poor socioeconomic conditions. Point being, both perceptions are valid, and it is sometimes hard to bring adults to consensus on defining trauma. I quickly noticed that providing TIC training helped with creating a common language, but I kept searching for a program where people could come together through a shared lens of compassion and put TIC into action in a more tangible way. I had heard about a program that connected law enforcement to schools for the purpose of sending a quick alert of a student's ACE exposure to their school. A Google search later, I found West Virginia's Handle With Care (HWC) website and began working with Andrea Darr,[32] Co-Founder of Handle With Care shortly after.

HWC is a quick-response effort to support students after their traumatic experiences and facilitate cross-systems professionals in working together to make a difference. To me, this program has literally been a door opener into TIC for our kids in the various counties in Ohio. Why? Because it makes perfect sense. People grab onto this program because no matter what your background, you can think of some circumstance where HWC can help a child. Even if the circumstance is not your own experience as a child, everyone can think of someone they know who has been affected by trauma.

After I learned about HWC, I was talking to a woman about the concept, and she simply said, "Wow that would have been helpful for me." She shared that as a child, she and her siblings had to be removed from her family and immediately put into the care of other family members. The next day at school, not wanting to share her story, she

---

[32] West Virginia Center for Children's Justice. Retrieved 1-12-23, from http://www.handlewithcarewv.org/contact.php

simply asked the teacher for an extension on her English paper and was told she would fail if she did not complete the assignment in the expected timeframe. The woman recalls that she was devastated, and I cannot help but think that teacher would have had a different response had she known the reason for the student's request. Instead of compassion, that child had trauma upon trauma stacked upon her that she still remembered many years later. The sad fact is, while we know teachers care deeply for their students, we also know that it can be impossible to decipher a true request from an excuse or know the circumstances of 25–200 students at one time. That is the benefit of HWC; it is communication that can make the difference!

I often refer to our law enforcement, school staff, and community partners as "care-ers." We chose different careers, but with the common theme of caring and wanting to make a difference. That commonality makes HWC an easy, "Yes!" I have heard countless stories from first responders and school staff about times when a notice would have been a great tool. Stories of children placed into foster care after a parent is arrested, stories of students struggling to meet school expectations only to learn days later that the students were evicted and were homeless, stories of students witnessing and experiencing domestic violence. There are too many stories like these; they are the reasons I love this program.

Perfect Timing

We were lucky in Ohio; we had perfect timing for implementation. In 2019, I connected with Andrea Darr[33] with the goal of implementing in one county. Not long after, I began receiving requests from nearby counties for more information and support. Maybe a teacher friend told another teacher friend, maybe there was a write-up in the local paper; in whatever method that communication happened, it happened very naturally. My one county effort had grown to about a dozen when the momentum brought HWC to the attention of the Ohio Department

---

[33] West Virginia Center for Children's Justice, Handle With Care, Contact Us. Retrieved 3-15-23, from http://www.handlewithcarewv.org/contact.php

of Mental Health and Addiction Services[34] (OMHAS). In early 2020, Hopewell Health Centers[35] officially partnered with OMHAS, and they funded the OhioHWC Lead position.

Now, as the OhioHWC State Lead (via Hopewell), I support counties throughout Ohio in their efforts to implement the OhioHWC program by providing consultation, training, and resources. Our goal is successful HWC programs promoting trauma-informed practices and creating school environments where all students can learn to the best of their abilities. OhioHWC aims to create communities where teachers and first responders feel valued, children are handled with care, and resilience is built through relationships.

While the Covid-19 pandemic played a distinct role in our statewide kickoff in March 2020, we moved forward with one virtual, statewide, informative training followed by five regional virtual trainings through the summer of that same year. Three years after our formal effort began, nearly all of Ohio's 88 counties are aware of the HWC program, over 40 are working toward implementation and more than a dozen are actively utilizing the program. Our goal is statewide implementation, working with each individual county on their timeline.

Statewide Outreach—Community Word of Mouth

While mandated HWC participation via legislation has been discussed and has potential benefits in settling concerns around legality and confidentiality that arise from time to time, we are moving along quickly without a mandate in place. Our approach has been a mix of statewide outreach and community word of mouth—a combination that is quickly helping us reach our goal. When inspiration catches on in a county, there is no stopping the momentum and often the spark jumps into other counties.

---

[34] Ohio Department of Mental Health and Addiction Services. Retrieved 3-6-23, from https://mha.ohio.gov/

[35] Hopewell Health Centers. Retrieved 3-6-23, from https://www.hopewell health.org/

Depending on the size of the county, there are advantages and disadvantages when implementing the HWC program. Here in Ohio, we have more than 600 school districts and each of them has its own superintendent. It is not uncommon to have a county that has a handful of school districts and a neighboring county that has a dozen districts. That means, multiple parties in leadership positions. For example: Cuyahoga County has 34 public school districts (therefore, 34 superintendents) and Vinton County has one district. Implementation is very different in those two counties.

County size also plays a role in implementation that can cause hurdles to maneuver around because of the number of first responders. For example, reporting in Franklin County where the population is 333,827,527[36] compared to reporting in Vinton County where the population is 12,696[37] are two very different systems. Therefore, reporting varies depending on the size of the county. Larger counties can often utilize different reporting systems due to their resources, where smaller counties have fewer staff and IT options. Each county reports as they see fit according to what works in their community, as long as the OhioHWC standards are met. Whether it be through dispatch or email, the job gets done, just differently.

Implementation

From the very beginning, we were strategic in implementation and purposeful in protecting the fidelity of the program. For example, if someone wants to start HWC, they work in collaboration with OhioHWC in order to gain permission to apply the model/name and program resources. We want to make sure every county follows the same basic model of fidelity developed by West Virginia, while allowing

---

[36] United States Census Bureau. Retrieved 3-6-23, from https://www.census.gov/quickfacts/fact/table/franklincountyohio,US/PST045222

[37] United States Census Bureau. Retrieved 1-4-23, from https://www.census.gov/quickfacts/fact/table/vintoncountyohio,US/PST045222,PST045221

flexibility to make the program the best fit locally for communities in Ohio.

Our County Coordinators are a vital part of the success of our program. Supported by OhioHWC through consultation, training, and resources, coordinators oversee implementation within their counties. They provide leadership, organization, support, and maintenance, while reporting progress (success and setbacks) to OhioHWC. Summarized, our coordinators follow the implementation outline:

1. Coordinator consultation meeting(s) with OhioHWC (ongoing)
2. County Partners Meeting
3. Training of Trainers
4. School Staff & First Responder Trainings
5. Program Launch: Notices & First Responder Visits
6. Data Reporting to OhioHWC

When a professional expresses interest in implementing the OhioHWC model in their area, we start by sharing introductory resources and then schedule an informational meeting. This usually is a one-hour consultation about the program. If they choose to move forward as a County Coordinator, the next step is the county Partners Meeting where attendees (leadership from first responder agencies, school districts, and other community agencies) learn about the program. The follow-up survey includes the question, "Do you support the implementation of HWC in your county?" The answer to that question has been "Yes" with an average rate of 99% agreement across Ohio's counties.

After the initial meeting, Coordinator's guide partnering agencies through the training phase and into active implementation. This process can be done two ways. The first way to implement is county-wide with all districts and corresponding first responder agencies training and launching simultaneously. The second way is through what we call a "rolling launch" where districts/communities come on board based on interest or timing.

Ohio utilizes a Training of Trainers model to meet the training needs. We work with district and department volunteers to train their colleagues and work with their County HWC Coordinator to move through the process. That being said, each county has to meet program fidelity, but we work with them to adjust implementation to fit their individual community needs—we promote fidelity *and* flexibility!

The Training of Trainer approach means a coordinator could have multiple volunteers, few, or even none. At one opening meeting, the county had 6 districts and there were 58 partners in attendance. The coordinator asked for training volunteers and 65 people came to the Training of Trainers meeting. This coordinator went from being a team of 1 to a team of 65 people helping to implement the program. Some coordinators, especially those in smaller counties, prefer to provide all trainings themselves or work with a much smaller training team to simplify. This aspect is based on coordinator preference and county/community need. The point being, the coordinator has the ability to ask for volunteers to assist in the trainings, and in fact, we find this works best.

When interested parties volunteer to assist in training their colleagues, colleagues listen. Firefighters listen to firefighters. Teachers listen to teachers. Police officers listen to other police officers. The coordinator can go in and train, but if the sheriff is standing in front of the other officers, there is a power dynamic that we cannot duplicate. Same situation if the principal is standing in front of the teachers, their presence makes a difference with "buy-in" of the program which creates a common mindset in place from the beginning. After one training I conducted, the sheriff stood up and said, "Okay you heard what she said, now I'm going to tell you in simple terms how to make that happen." They all listened.

The time required for full program implementation varies, but our average in Ohio is six months to one year. We distinguish these different phases of implementation by color: yellow for interest, green is the development phase, and blue for programs that are active. The coordinator oversees development and then announces the program's transition to active status. This signals that it is time for first responders to utilize their system to send the HWC notices to participating districts. There are two primary requirements for achieving active status: First, all staff involved in sending or receiving a HWC notice must have completed the required training, and second, a schedule allowing first responders to visit schools is in place.

Why first responder visits? First responder visits to schools are opportunities for connection and resilience-building through frequent interactions with a variety of first responders. If a student's main interaction with police/first responders occurs during a traumatic event, they may feel frightened and mistrustful during subsequent contact. The program's first responder visits allow students the opportunity to develop a new perspective and hopefully new relationships, all within the school setting where students are more likely to feel safe.

Where We Stand Today

We invite County Coordinators to a monthly meeting to provide updates and support. At the last virtual meeting, I was moved while looking at the screen. For some people, HWC is their job; they get paid to implement the program. Other people get a stipend and squeeze the time out of their regular workday to oversee the program. Some are working to implement HWC without any additional incentives. All of the people on that screen were just trying to make a positive difference in the world, and it is my privilege to work alongside them.

Today, we have over 40 counties in the implementation process and 86 of our 88 counties have expressed an interest in the program. There are 12 counties actively implementing HWC and another 30 have shown interest. By the time this book is published, I am sure those numbers will change, but the bottom line is, we are well on our way to statewide implementation, one unique county at a time.

Chapter 4

How to Implement Handle With Care in Your School

Sara Kettwig, School Safety Specialist, South Dakota
Brett.Garland@state.sd.us

I was a teacher for 20 years. During one of my last years of teaching first grade, I had a young boy, and midway through the year, I noticed a change in his demeanor in my classroom. This student eventually cried out to me that he was being abused by his half-brother. School became his safe place. I was at a loss for how to help this boy except to let him sleep as he was so tired when he walked through my door in the morning. I then worked with him on schoolwork when we could.

I had bought a book that I read after having this boy called "Lost at School"[38] that helped me to understand a very simple concept: kids tell you what they need. In his book, Dr. Greene cited an example of a boy in a second-grade classroom that had a tantrum every day in math. He was inconsolable until finally the teacher asked what could be done to stop his behavior. He said simply, "You don't let us finish the math game. You make us put it away every day before there is an ending. How can it be a game if there is no winner?" The teacher brainstormed

---

[38] Greene, R. (2014). *Lost at school: Why our kids with behavioral challenges are falling through the cracks and how we can help them.* Scribner.

with the boy and they decided at the end of class to put the board on a shelf so he could continue it at the end of last period during free time. No more tantrums; problem solved. Not only do you have to ask what is wrong, you must listen.

After this experience, I set out to change my classroom. I began to teach myself about creating a trauma sensitive classroom for all kids. Low lights, low stress, rules of respect, and lessons on how to calm yourself by using your words or removing yourself to a quiet place. When I changed my classroom, my negative classroom behaviors disappeared. We had a plan in place and the kids knew the plan. That year was hard, but I owe that little boy everything because he changed how I saw kids in my class, in my school, in the world. He changed my life as a teacher and as a person.

When I changed careers and became a School Safety Specialist for our state, I made it my mission to learn about trauma informed classrooms and share that information with as many teachers as I could. I heard about Handle With Care (HWC) when I was in Rapid City one month after starting my new job and quickly contacted Andrea Darr[39] to ask about the program. My mission was to do everything in my power to bring this program to my state of South Dakota. My motivation—I wished I would have known about HWC while I was still teaching, especially because of that one little boy in my first-grade classroom.

Today, we are moving full speed ahead, but very differently than other states. Here in small town, rural America, what other people call counties, we call communities. Because our state is extremely rural, there is a great deal of "cross-over" between school, sheriff departments, and emergency first responders. Rather than limiting areas to districts, we cross borders to encompass the entire community area. Borders are limiting while communities can serve based on need. For example: Where I live there are 6 schools in the county, but we don't centralize our schools by county so there are 6 different HWC programs, yet some of them would include some of the same law enforcement. So

---

[39]   West Virginia Center for Children's Justice, Contact Us. Retrieved 3-29-23, from http://www.handlewithcarewv.org/contact.php

many times when I sit in on the national Zoom call that Andrea Darr conducts monthly, I think to myself "that would never work in our state" and here is why. The Midwest is different.

The South Dakota Way

South Dakota is a non-regulatory state which simply means no one tells you what to do. To say that we would mandate HWC in our state would probably never happen. Our thought is, when people hear about this program and see what it does for children, they will want to bring it to their community. Implementation of this program would be a grassroots effort by people who want the program because they know it is what is best for kids. Every community works very differently and this is why I love this program; you make it your own. I never tell any person how to run the program, I just get them started and offer guidance and support.

Our mission is to bring HWC to the entire state, one school at a time. To date, we have 20 communities that are in the process and more that are showing interest. If schools are interested, I come in and provide information on HWC and to support that community to get the program up and running. I want them to own their program. I can support them when there are questions, but the program belongs to that individual community.

I begin to support them when they form their stakeholder's group. I have schools work with the police and first responders first because, as I tell the schools, if they do not have the support and complete buy-in from the police department and first responders, they will never have an effective program. There is no program without them. That being said, we never have a problem getting police and first responders on board. As a matter of fact, I hear repeatedly from officers that this is the perfect thing for our kids and they jump on the chance to start the program. Why? Prior to this program, the deputies were forced to walk away from a traumatic scene not knowing if anyone would be there to comfort the kids who were in that home. HWC closes that chapter for them. Now they know someone at school is looking after those children, it alleviates a common stressor for those deputies.

Once Law Enforcement and First Responders are on board, the training can begin. That is my passion.

HWC in the Schools in South Dakota

My job as School Safety Specialist with HWC simply put is for support. When I receive a phone call from a community interested in information about the HWC program, I set up a face-to-face meeting to answer any questions they have. Usually, I meet with the very people who made the phone call and we have a very casual Q & A session. I really want them to ask all the hard questions because if they are interested enough to make contact, they are usually the ones who are the strongest advocates for the program. My thought is, if I answer all their questions, they can in turn be empowered to promote the program in their community and have the confidence that they know the answers to questions that may be asked of them. We talk about all the requirements of the program based on the fidelity of the West Virginia HWC program[40] and the amount of work involved to set up a successful program. Although the program is simple, it takes organization and effort to successfully implement it in your community. After the initial meeting, I wait for them to call me when they have decided to implement the program.

When the community has decided to move forward, they set up a stakeholders meeting. This board can consist of any number of people, and it is interesting the differences between membership in each community. Along with the required representatives from school and emergency responders, you could have anyone from doctors to politicians serving on the board. Because South Dakota is very rural

---

[40] West Virginia Center for Children's Justice, How to get HWC Started in my County. Retrieved 3-27-23, from http://www.handlewithcarewv.org/get-hwc-started.php

and the communities are small, you could see a mayor serving next to a city council member; it is completely up to the community.

I hold every one of the stakeholders' meetings in person. We have a one-hour presentation followed by a Q & A session. I try to guide the members to make decisions as to who will be responsible for the "nitty gritty" part of HWC implementation by completing a Work Plan that they can follow to show what duties need to be performed, when, and by whom. If the community decides to follow this outline, it helps to lay out exactly who is responsible for what duty and a timeline to follow. I got the idea for the Work Plan from the first school in SD to implement HWC. After the stakeholders meeting, they start working on their program and I slowly walk away. Eventually, I am just there for support and to answer questions. I try to make everything as simple as possible for the communities as they plan their program; they have enough on their plate. I give them all the MOUs, Work Plan, newspaper articles, training for staff, and they can use it or create their own.

The schools then provide the trauma training that we recommend; which includes three hours of trauma training for all staff. That means not only teachers and administrators, but custodians, bus drivers, secretaries, and any personnel who work at the school. If, during this training they do not have a trained ACE's trainer, I connect them with one. I also recommend the Brain Architecture Game[41] to be played at a future in-service. I have seen some amazing results of people changing their way of thinking by playing this game. When teachers have not been exposed to trauma training, they just don't always get the impact that trauma can have on a child. This game helps change that mindset. Some communities include book studies to support ACEs training.

---

41   Center on Developing Child, Harvard University, The Brain Architecture Game. Retrieved 3-27-23, from https://developingchild.harvard.edu/resources/the-brain-architecture-game/

Two books that I usually recommend are Lost at School[42] and Help for Billy[43] or anything by Bruce Perry or John Greene.

When the notification plan is in place and all key players have been completely trained, it is time to start. It has been described as like being on the edge of a cliff and taking a leap of faith. As frightening as that sounds, you jump in and sink or swim. If the community is doing the plan for a month and minimal tips are being received or there is confusion on any level at the school, we reconvene the stakeholders. The life jacket you always have is the safety net of the stakeholders to go back and revise the process. If called upon, I can go back in as support to go over the plan and suggest any improvements. The most recent school I am working with has reported their initial plan is working flawlessly and that is the goal.

State Support of HWC

In this, the first full year of implementation, that is how I have run the program. I have kept some things and changed so many things. Every time I go to a conference, I do my best to give and take the best practices of this program. I always try to present so I can share what we have learned in SD. My goal each time I adjust our program is to make HWC as easy as possible to implement. After all, HWC is my job, but for the teachers and school personnel, it is just one small thing on their very full plate. This program communicates the information that a student may have been traumatized and to handle that child with care. Simple program, big results.

Since we are so new to the program, we have not done anything with the data except to see if the program is working and if they need additional support or training. As we move on in the program, we will move forward with this as well. For now, some of the schools are using

---

[42] Greene, R. W. (2014). *Lost at school: Why our kids with behavioral challenges are falling through the cracks and how we can help them.* Simon and Schuster.

[43] Forbes, H. T. (2012). *Help for Billy: A beyond consequences approach to helping challenging children in the classroom.* Beyond Consequences Institute.

the Excel Spreadsheet that the West Virginia Center for Children's Justice[44] Handle With Care program supports. No names are included, but various data are collected. To me, the most important thing you can gather is if there are repeated notices for the same child and when that report is happening. For instance, if Johnny is getting a HWC tip at the end of every month, why is that? Does the money run out at the end of the month at Johnny's house? Is stress high because rent is due or there is no money for food? Does that family need help? Or is Sasha getting a HWC tip every other Friday because the night before is payday and a parent is out with their friends? If there are patterns, what can we do to help that child and their family? If the child does not seek help, maybe it is just providing a quiet place for Sasha every other Friday morning until she regulates herself into the school day. Maybe it is a granola bar in the a.m. for Johnny, a good lunch, and a bag dinner to take home the last week of the month. The point is, if you know something is happening, you can provide targeted grace precisely when that child needs it the most.

If a community is not ready to start HWC now, that is okay. My goal is to get everyone on board. Will that happen? I hope eventually. The key here is to scaffold people to understand trauma. My friend is a good example. She is a good person, but like so many, she did not want to believe that really bad things happened in her community, or maybe deep down she knew, but didn't want to believe it. One day out of the blue she emailed me and said, "I want to look into starting HWC in my community." Apparently, she had a little girl in her office who was having a rough day and she shared that her dad had cut his ankle bracelet off and there was a great deal that went on in her household the night before she came to school. My friend immediately realized had they been better informed, they would have been better prepared when this child came to school instead of ending up in her office. It will take individual awareness like that example for this program to spread.

---

44   West Virginia Center for Children's Justice, Andrea Darr. Retrieved 3-28-23, from http://www.handlewithcarewv.org/

Many of our leads come from the help of our Department of Education.[45] They are extremely supportive of this program and when they do an email push, I received multiple calls from people. When they call out, people listen. Word of mouth is also a major piece of the puzzle in spreading information about this program in this state because our communities are so tight knit. People know what is going on in each community so if a neighboring school is implementing HWC, the school next door watches it unfold and soon makes a call.

Unfortunately, now it is probably my office that is holding up further expansion because of the snow! We have multiple schools that have initiated contact and are waiting for my attendance at Q & A's or stakeholder's meetings. When you live here, the weather can block the best laid plans. There are multiple schools wanting to train this summer and kick off next school year and I have every expectation that they will do just that.

The fabulous thing about this program is that it is a grassroots effort that you make work for your individual community. I come in to get the community started and then it is 100% up to them. This is not about the state telling local communities how to run their program. Fidelity is important nationally, answering questions and empowerment is important for state support, but implementation is local. In this state, to say, "You have to do it this way," would be a mistake here. You need your own people chosen locally who have a stake in the failure or success of programming in order to have ownership. It makes me proud that so many people are showing so much interest after only one year.

Now

Being a teacher, I have a special place in my heart to make sure that all our caregivers in this field are fully aware of the baggage that kids carry around because of trauma. Although we cannot control

---

[45]   South Dakota Department of Education, Special Education, DOE Highlights, Coming Soon Handle with Care Program. Retrieved 3-28-23, from https://doe.sd.gov/sped/documents/DirectorsCalls/1221-newsletter.pdf

homelife, we can control our classroom atmosphere. My personal goal is to eventually have trauma training for all teachers. Of course, training costs money and takes time and there are obstacles to overcome, yet I know it would make such a difference in our state. I envision an initial informational training about trauma informed classrooms and then quick implementation tips to offer continual support and real conversations about big questions.

When teachers have been trained in trauma, the very next thing they want to know is, "How do I address this in the classroom?" That is when we could offer continual, quick tips of support. Why do kids tolerate stress differently? Discuss why the same thing can happen to two different kids and the reaction on their part is completely different. How does being sent to the office affect a kid who was traumatized the night before? Discuss trauma informed care that begins and ends in the classroom (Red, yellow, green lights; working as an informed team where all students are aware of their aggravation level and how to communicate that emotion and later how to control it). Teachers need tools in their belt to build an environment that is safe and secure for all kids to learn and grow, because it is not about us—it is about the kids. How are we going to get them to feel successful, every single day, as long as we have them in our care?

It is a quest we continue in this great state, one school at a time.

Chapter 5

How to Implement Handle With Care in Your Law Enforcement Agency

Lieutenant Veto Mentzell,
Harford County Sheriff's Office, Maryland
Mentzellv@harfordsheriff.org

When I started as the Program Director of our Child Advocacy Center (CAC), I had no idea what ACEs even meant. Later I thought, "How could I have never heard of this?" It was mid-2016 and the information about this study was just starting to trickle out. When I began to investigate the research, I knew that it addressed many questions that needed to be answered and I felt strongly that we all had a role to play. I took my part very seriously and joined others from around our state[46] to become an ACE Interface Master Trainer.[47]

---

[46]   Maryland The Daily Record, "Child Advocacy Groups Launch ACE Interface Project." Retrieved 12-28-22, from https://thedailyrecord.com/2018/01/04/child-advocacy-groups-launch-ace-interface-project/?utm_source=pocket_reader

[47]   Master Trainer Education, The ACE Interface Train the Master Trainer Program. Retrieved 12-22-22, from https://www.aceinterface.com/MTE.html#

In April 2017, the CAC hosted a public screening of the film "Resilience"[48] in recognition of National Child Abuse Prevention Month. At the screening, we invited those in attendance to join the follow-up discussion. The next month, myself and others started a committee made up of multidisciplinary members and called ourselves the Harford County ACE's steering committee. We welcomed anyone willing to join and we were made up of social workers, educators, administrators, criminal justice professionals, first responders, public health officials, medical and mental health providers, victim advocates, faith community, and private citizens. Our primary focus was on reducing childhood abuse, neglect, and dysfunction in our community.

It was during this point of researching information for our committee, I came across a little program called Handle With Care (HWC), which had been first developed in West Virginia.[49] Almost at that first meeting, we decided to focus our attention on bringing the HWC program to our county. Why? Honestly it was "low hanging fruit," so to speak; easy to implement and little to no cost—and we believed in it. HWC sounded somewhat similar to our own Trauma Recognition and Coordination program (TRAC), but on a larger scale. At the time, we had no idea the impact that this program would have on our community, our county, and now our state of Maryland.

From there, the program just took off. During one unrelated high school presentation, we mentioned HWC and one of the students decided to do her capstone project on the program. She did research during her senior year and collected, collated, and presented her findings. Her presentation was so well loved, it eventually garnered the attention of the Governor's Office of Crime Control and Prevention[50] (GOCCP), and before we knew it, we found ourselves standing beside her as she presented at their offices in Crownsville. The GOCCP had begun

---

48   KPJR Films, *Resilience, The Biology of Stress and the Science of Hope*. Retrieved 12-22-22, from https://kpjrfilms.co/resilience/request-resilience/

49   West Virginia Center for Children's Justice. http://www.handlewithcarewv.org/

50   Maryland, Governor's Office of Crime Control and Prevention, Youth, and Victim Services. Retrieved 2-17-23, from http://goccp.maryland.gov/

taking an interest and was helping connect different Maryland counties who were implementing the program. Andrea Darr, Co-Founder of Handle With Care,[51] attended this presentation and we were later invited to present at the HWC Conference in West Virginia.

The Pilot Program

Once the steering committee decided to focus on HWC for our county, it was almost a year later that we signed a Memorandum of Understanding (MOU) between the Sheriff's Office and the public school system to begin implementing our pilot program. Joppatowne High School[52] and the five schools that fed into it were targeted as pilot schools and we trained over 400 teachers from all 6 schools in one unprecedented, large group.

Pilot training for the schools was a 2-hour ACE Interface Presentation and detailed information on HWC. Immediately after implementing the pilot, we saw the need for HWC in more and more schools. We began responding to each non-pilot school, to get teachers and staff trained. With the help of the public schools, we eventually filmed and edited one of these sessions to produce a training video for the rest of the schools in the county. The rollout of our pilot couldn't have been timed better because the new Director of Student Support Services was already planning to bring trauma-informed response system-wide. After the pilot, the public schools would go on to provide three comprehensive training events on trauma-informed response for all teachers and staff.

Our law enforcement pilot training started out very different. The buy-in was easy. Our officers are the first line of defense, and this program is an easy sell. They are already responding to these calls for service anyway, so HWC is not a heavy lift for them. However, unlike the teacher training, we were up against time and implementation deadlines so I had to fit all of the information into a 15-minute presentation

---

[51]   West Virginia Center for Children's Justice – Contact Us. http://www. handlewithcarewv.org/contact.php

[52]   Joppatowne High School. Retrieved 12-22, from https://johs.ss18.sharpschool.com/

during roll call. Needless to say, this turned out to be challenging. At the time, the annual in-service schedule had already been set and we felt that just offering on demand training videos was not enough support to implement the pilot with any fidelity.

Once in-person training was decided, the logistics were a bit tedious with day, evening, and midnight shift roll calls 2–3 times a week to make sure all deputies on opposing squads were impacted. As the pilot expanded, we also had to train all of the officers from the 3 allied police departments in our jurisdiction, as well as the troopers from our local state police barrack.

Training for Established Law Enforcement

We take training for law enforcement very seriously. Why? When a child is not safe at home, their developing brains will adapt to that lack of safety with behaviors that can cause disciplinary actions in school. Over time when there is repeated discipline, kids may eventually flunk out, drop out, or be kicked out. A child who is forced out of school generally has nowhere else to go and may eventually find themselves in the criminal justice system. Once there, it is hard to break free. So, they may continue on this path until adulthood where they repeat these same mistakes with their own children and the cycle begins all over again.

Officers who have been on this job for any amount of time can name the repeat offender families in our community. It is a common experience. We came into this job arresting the grandparents and parents and leave this job arresting the children, grandchildren, and great grandchildren. If we want to break this cycle, we must use a proactive approach. If we can help schools deter negative behavior, we can help children succeed in school. Success in school can aid success in life. That is what HWC can do for kids, families, and communities.

Training for law enforcement already in the field consists of roll call training and follow-up on that initial training during our annual in-service where we can spend a little more time on the subject. One tool we utilize during roll call training is the ACEs Primer video (bonus content from the film "Resilience"[53]) as it fits our needs perfectly for distilling the ACEs science into a 5-minute explanation. Also included in the training is a video of Chief Deputy Wade Shambaugh from The Morgan County Sheriff's Office speaking about HWC as an introduction. Officers tend to listen to fellow officers, especially when they speak with experience. I thought law enforcement officers would relate to him when he says:

> In law enforcement we get approached to participate in a lot of programs. A lot of stuff is hard to implement or expensive or not really that beneficial. Sometimes quite frankly, it's just to make the public feel good and doesn't really benefit anybody. Handle With Care Program is not one of those.[54]

We didn't invent these videos; we were just lucky enough to find them and fortunate to be able to put them to use. Another available resource to utilize is Andrea Darr.[55] Andrea and her team are always willing to share resources and now they have even produced their own 9-minute roll call video.[56] Unfortunately, that was not available at the time of our pilot.

In addition to the two videos, we also go over several PowerPoint slides to bring our training home. We discuss how trauma in children can "turn off the learning switch" and why it is important law enforcement officers do our part to mitigate any additional trauma. We stress the importance of identifying when there are children present. Are there

---

[53]   KPJR Films, Resilience, The Biology of Stress and the Science of Hope. Retrieved 12-22-22, from http://kpjrfilms.co/resilience/bonus-content/

[54]   Wade Shambaugh Speaking on Handle with Care program. https://www.youtube.com/watch?v=sygYyctwjwk&t=18s

[55]   West Virginia Center for Children's Justice, Handle with Care for Law Enforcement. Retrieved on 2-30-22, from http://www.handlewithcarewv.org/law-enforcement-protocol.php

[56]   Handle With Care - Roll Call Video. https://vimeo.com/380526937?embedded=true&source=vimeo_logo&owner=70337135

bikes in the driveway? Are there toys in the yard or inside the house? If the parents say the kids are upstairs asleep, are they really sleeping through domestic violence? If dad leaves or mom is arrested the night before, kids can be tired or worried or want to use their phone to stay connected to their parents or siblings. These stressors may manifest in negative behaviors at school that could lead to punishment. When the reaction to an exposure to trauma is misunderstood and treated as a discipline problem, trauma is compounded. A simple HWC notice can help to avoid this from happening.

The notice we created is a simple email with the child's name, age or date of birth, and school. No other information is provided. In our world, the simpler the better, so the notice is straightforward and easy to access. The emails go to designated members of the public schools' Student Support Services Division, who in turn ensure the notice is provided to that child's teacher(s) before the bell rings the next day. The notices are not retained or tracked and do not become part of the child's permanent record. We do not attach copies of police reports or provide any details regarding the incident that prompted the notice. It could be anything from a family member being arrested or witnessing community violence, to a car accident or a medical emergency. The schools are not entitled to that information, nor do they need it in order to help the child. We are simply giving the school a heads up that a particular student may need a little more support that day. The schools actually have the more difficult task; our part is an email.

School staff are trained not to take any action solely on our notice. Any assistance they provide is predicated on the child's behavior. Some children already have the family or community support necessary to help them be resilient in the face of a traumatic event and do not need our help. Other children need more support. Maybe they take a nap in the nurse's office and only miss a few hours of the school day rather than the whole day. Maybe a test gets postponed, or they are given an extra day to turn in their homework. Maybe they get a little more one-on-one support from their teacher. The point is a traumatic event is not treated as a discipline problem and that student is given the opportunity to succeed. Once you realize what this program can accomplish through a simple email, implementing it is a no brainer—although sometimes it is.

I remember during one presentation a commander gave me a hard time. His contentious questioning went on throughout the training. I felt prepared with good responses and tried to let my support of HWC shine through. The debate did make for some spirited discussion and was nonetheless engaging, so I thought nothing more of it. Later that night, he called me to apologize. The information had really gotten under his skin. When he took time to think it through, he said, "I am not sure this will work, but I want to help you do it." Over time he became an advocate for the program and used his influence to bring us a wider audience in the community. I call that a win.

Once we got through the initial rollout, our focus shifted to maintaining the success of the program through fidelity to the model and ongoing training. Every couple of years we go back over the HWC training with veteran officers during the mandatory in-service block on child maltreatment. However, we have placed a particular emphasis on training our next generation of law enforcement.

New Recruits

Years ago, when I entered the Training Academy as a new recruit, it was like, "Oh you criminal justice majors, forget all that stuff they taught you in college; this is what you really need to know." Then once I graduated the Training Academy and entered Field Training my Field Training Officer (FTO) would say, "Forget all of that stuff they taught you in the Training Academy; this is what you really need to know." And then when I passed Field Training and joined a shift my first Commander would say, "Forget all that stuff your FTO showed you; this is what you really need to know" and so on. The truth is that it is all as equally important as it is hard to retain. In the 7 months you have with new recruits, there is so much to go over that not everything can stick (which is why Field Training and good supervision become so important later). However, there are things that can make a lasting impression and we want this to be one of them, because this is something that can positively impact everything they will do as a law enforcement officer.

When I began as Program Director of the CAC, new recruits only received about a half day of child maltreatment training—not good enough. Now they receive two and half days. The last half day is devoted entirely to developmental adversity. New recruits watch the 1-hour "Resilience" film, receive a 2-hour ACE Interface presentation, and an additional presentation on HWC. Through facilitated discussion, there are multiple opportunities for them to absorb and process this information. This coming year I am adding an interactive game[57] to the training in which the new recruits can participate to provide more hands-on learning. Their overall response is usually, "What can I do about this? How can I help?" One answer is HWC. Law, policy, scene safety, and sound tactics are always going to come first, but once they are addressed, you can circle back to help a child.

Most new hires will tell you they got into this line of work to help people. HWC is one way we can do that. We currently see the highest rate of compliance and fidelity to the HWC program from our newer deputies. I hope that is because for many this becomes a seminal training that stays with them their whole career. The main drive behind any of our presentations is passion. I think officers want to know that you weren't just assigned to this, but that this program works, and you believe in it. Bottom line: who doesn't want to help kids?

Today

So where do things stand now? Our original ACEs steering committee no longer meets. Unfortunately, we all had full-time jobs and we just couldn't sustain the obligation. But that did not stop or interfere with the momentum that this effort had already built. There is now grant funding available to sustain these projects and many counties

---

[57]   The Brain Architecture Game. Retrieved 12-28-22, from https://dev. thebrainarchitecturegame.com/

have hired someone to be their ACEs coordinator. In our county, grant funding was given to a local private non-profit for this effort and there is still some grassroots work being done ad hoc.

HWC has been fully implemented in all of our public schools and with all of the law enforcement agencies in our county. Although our group is a little more splintered, we are still pushing HWC forward. Most recently we have been working to bring on Fire/EMS for sending notices, and we have discussed expanding HWC beyond the public school system to private schools, daycares, and before/after school programs.

HWC Maryland is also alive and well with the full attention of the Governor's Office for eventual state-wide implementation. There is now a HWC Maryland website with information about the program (modeled after HWC West Virginia's website). We contribute monthly statistics which are posted to their data dashboard.[58]

So far, the feedback we have received is positive. Through VOCA[59] grant funding, we did an early program evaluation of our pilot which documented an increased familiarity with ACEs and the impact of trauma in both teachers and law enforcement officers exposed to the training. The high school student's capstone project which was previously mentioned looked at the program from the viewpoint of a student. Overwhelmingly the student body saw value in this program and we found worth in representing the opinions of our youth in our data collection. The program is continuously evolving based on feedback.

We also relentlessly follow-up to ensure the program is operating smoothly. I get a copy of every HWC notice that is sent. This serves a two-fold purpose. First, I can thank the officer for sending the email. I have heard from many officers that when a call is made and Child Protective Services is involved, they never hear back. "We never know

---

[58]   Handle With Care Maryland. Retrieved 12-28-22, from https://handlewithcaremd.org/hwc-data.php

[59]   Office for Victims of Crime (VOCA). Retrieved 2-17-23, from https://goccp.maryland.gov/grants/programs/voca/

what happened to the kid" has been a repeated complaint. Responding to every notice is a small way to let the officer know that their notice was received, and that child was cared for the next day at school. That is big. Second, once in a while someone will make a mistake and attach more information than they are supposed to send. I can thank them for sending the notice and then remind them of the protocol that only the child's name, age or date of birth, and school are included in the HWC notice.

Refresher emails are sent periodically with the Quick Reference sheet we developed. This reference includes information about HWC on one side and helpful tips on how to respond to kids who have experienced trauma on the other side. The refresher emails also remind officers to send notices during winter, spring and summer breaks, holidays, and on weekends. It keeps people in the habit of sending the notices and informs the schools of events while they were not in session. Kids can bring a lot of baggage with them when they come back from break.

I can tell you that I am grateful for the partners who walked with me on this journey. It is not uncommon for me to get calls from people all over the country asking how we started this program, and I am always happy to answer any questions. To me, it was obvious that we had to do this. All it took was some elbow grease, working together, and following up. I'm not saying there are no obstacles—there are, but in the end, we all work together in the best interest of this program to help kids. I see this as a long-term investment, so that in one generation HWC and incorporating the concepts of developmental adversity will just be the norm. That is the goal.

About the Author

Wendy L. Samford, Ph.D., worked in the K-12 setting as an administrator for 13 years, higher education for 8 years, and has been writing for 9 years. Her passion lies in working to support children of all ages, no matter where that direction may lead. This, her fifth book, *How to Handle With Care*, is a beautiful tribute to a program near and dear to her heart. Her mission remains consistent in all her books: to do her best to advocate for children in order to make a positive difference in their lives, according to God's will. Wendy is happily married and has four great kids and one awesome granddaughter.

Contact the Author:
Website: www.WSamford.com
Email: Wendy@WSamford.com
Facebook: facebook.com/WendySamfordAuthor/